Decorating *for the* first time®

Decorating *for the* first time®

Eileen Cannon Paulin

Sterling Publishing Co., Inc. New York
A Sterling/Chapelle Book

Chapelle, Ltd.:
Jo Packham, Sara Toliver, Cindy Stoeckl
Editor: Jennifer Luman
Book Layout: Pinnacle Marketing Communications, Inc.
Copy Editor: Marilyn Goff

Staff: Kelly Ashkettle, Areta Bingham, Anne Bruns, Donna Chambers,
    Emily Frandsen, Karla Haberstich, Lana Hall, Susan Jorgensen,
    Melissa Maynard, Barbara Milburn, Lecia Monsen, Suzy Skadburg,
    Kim Taylor, Desirée Wybrow

If you have any questions or comments, please contact:
Chapelle, Ltd., Inc., P.O. Box 9252, Ogden, UT 84409
(801) 621-2777 • (801) 621-2788 Fax
 e-mail: chapelle@chapelleltd.com
web site: www.chapelleltd.com

A Red Lips 4 Courage Book
Eileen Cannon Paulin, Rebecca Ittner, Catherine Risling

Red Lips 4 Courage Communications
8502 E. Chapman Ave., 303
Orange, CA 92869
e-mail: rl4courage@redlips4courage.com
web site: www.redlips4courage.com

   This volume is meant to stimulate craft ideas. If readers are unfamiliar or not proficient in a skill necessary to attempt a project, we urge that they refer to an instructional book specifically addressing the required technique.

Library of Congress Cataloging-in-Publication Data

Paulin, Eileen Cannon.
Decorating for the first time / Eileen Cannon Paulin.
p. cm.
"A Sterling/Chapelle Book."
Includes index.
ISBN 1-4027-0937-4
1. Interior decoration. I. Title.

NK2115.P
374 2004
747--dc22 2004004071 10 9 8 7 6 5 4 3 2 1

Published by Sterling Publishing Co., Inc.
387 Park Avenue South, New York, NY 10016
©2004 by Eileen Cannon Paulin
Distributed in Canada by Sterling Publishing
c/o Canadian Manda Group, 165 Dufferin Street,
Toronto, Ontario, Canada M6K 3H6
Distributed in Great Britain by Chrysalis Books Group PLC,
The Chrysalis Building, Bramley Road, London W10 6SP, England
Distributed in Australia by Capricorn Link (Australia) Pty. Ltd.
P. O. Box 704, Windsor, NSW 2756, Australia
Printed and Bound in China
All Rights Reserved
Sterling ISBN 1-4027-0937-4

In Tribute

To my husband Stephen, children Brendan and Sarah, and to my father David Cannon, whose support has enabled me to pursue my dreams. To Rebecca Ittner and Cathy Risling, without whom I would not have had the courage to put on red lips. To Jo Packham, who made it possible. And to the One who inspires all things.

Table of Contents

Introduction

Doing anything for the first time can be exciting, yet at the same time it can be overwhelming. Decorating is no exception. You've been looking forward to your own home and being able to make it unique to you.

Whether this first-time decorating project is in a rented apartment or a home you have purchased, what you are about to embark on will take time, money, and a great deal of thought. Above all, it should be fun and enjoyable. This is your chance to do things the way you want.

Don't be fooled into thinking that there are hard-and-fast rules about how you have to do things. When it comes to decorating, there is only one person's opinion that counts—yours. There are, of course, some tried-and-true guidelines. Most of them have been developed by people who have made numerous mistakes along the way. Don't let yourself be intimidated.

There's never been a better time to undertake a decorating project; sources are abundant. There is an overwhelming amount of information and countless places to go for products and ideas. If anything, you may find that there are too many places to turn for inspiration, and that your first step is getting a handle on how to get started.

Many books on decorating have been written, and it's likely you'll refer to many throughout your decorating process. Rather than wag a finger at you and tell you, "do this," or, "don't do that," we will equip you with the basics and give you an overview of each of the many decisions you will be making.

What you ultimately choose to do is up to you. After all, if there's one place in this world that you deserve to have the final say, it's in your own home.

Eileen Cannon Paulin

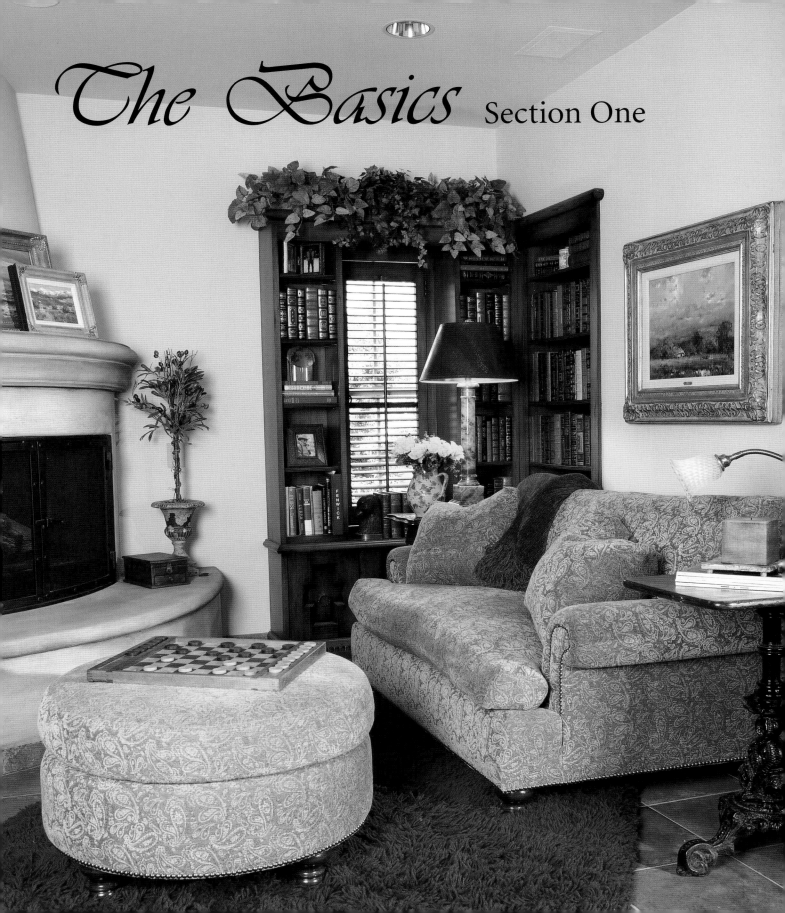

The Basics Section One

Home Sweet Decorated Home

Your home is personal. When you've finished decorating, it should be a reflection of you. Before getting carried away with the creative fun of a decorating project, you need to play business manager and take a look at some facts so that you don't waste your time and money.

Will I Stay or Will I Go?

Before spending time and money decorating your home, ask yourself how long you plan to live there. If you're renting an apartment, your decorating plan should center on furniture and window coverings that will move with you. If you've settled into a home you plan on spending years in, concentrate on the structure first and make improvements such as adding windows, built-in cabinets, and installing moldings before you start on fabrics and furniture.

After you decide which room you are going to decorate first, remove everything and start from scratch. Even take out the pieces you plan to keep. This way, you can better see the room's possibilities.

Mapping Out a Room

Decorating is like a journey—it's best to have a map. Purchase some graph paper, a metal ruler, and have plenty of pencils on hand. Decide on your own scale and convert your room measurements to the scale on the graph paper.

1. Draw a floor plan for the room, indicating overall room dimensions.

2. Indicate where windows and doors are and show their dimensions. Note whether doors open to the inside or outside of the room.

3. Decide what the focal point of the room will be. It may be a fireplace, a bay window, an architectural element, or a piece of furniture such as a piano. You'll want to group furniture around a focal point.

4. Leave room for general traffic patterns. The major traffic path should be 36" by 48" wide. Smaller traffic paths should be about 24". Be certain to allow room to open drawers and space for moving chairs in and out of a table with ease.

5. Measure the furniture pieces you want to use in the room. Cut out pieces of paper to represent each piece of furniture and to coordinate with this scale.

6. Create conversation areas by keeping groups of furniture close enough to each other so people can talk easily.

7. Put a table or ottoman near a chair; avoid leaving a chair by itself.

Budget

Once you get started decorating, you will not believe how quickly the money is spent. Take time to plan expenditures for each part of the project. Here are the major categories you need to consider, and what might be included in each.

DEMOLITION: Removal of old walls, wood floors, lighting, or cabinets. If you do this yourself, consider any tools you'll need to rent or purchase. Include cost for furniture moving, disposal of materials removed, and cleanup.

PREPARATION: Repairing walls, ceiling, or floors. Consider all costs for protecting existing parts of your home from dust and grit. This should include taping off other rooms with plastic, covering air vents, and laying a protective cover on floors and carpets.

PHYSICAL ALTERATIONS: Moving or adding walls, windows, doors, new wiring, lighting, electrical outlets, or a sound system.

FLOORS: Tile, wood, laminate, stone, or carpet. In addition to the material being installed, remember to include moisture barriers and slab sealing for wood, tile, and laminate floors. When installing carpet, purchase the best quality pad you can afford.

WINDOW COVERINGS: Draperies, valances, sheers, curtains, and blinds. Be certain to include all hardware. If you are making your own window coverings, include the cost of fabric and supplies.

LIGHTING: Fixtures, lamps, sconces, and any other lighting to be used in the room.

WALLS: Paint, wallpaper, or whatever treatment you choose.

FURNITURE: Tables, chairs, accent pieces, and upholstered pieces.

ACCESSORIES: Artwork, frames, and other table decor. Be sure to leave yourself some money to spend on accessorizing the room. It is usually the most enjoyable part of the project.

First-time Tip

Find out where the outlets are in your area that sell consignment furniture. Once a builder closes a set of models, the furniture is sent to a consignment center. While the selection is sometimes hit-and-miss, these outlets are filled with cost savings.

Working with an Interior Decorator

Depending on the scope of your decorating project, you may want to work with an interior decorator. In the long run, you may save money because of the sources a decorator has and the advice that will steer you clear of mistakes.

Carol Donayre Bugg, vice president of interior design for INTERIORS by Decorating Den, has extensive experience working with an array of clients including those decorating for the first time. She offers the following insights for choosing an interior decorator.

The proliferation of home decor cable TV shows and magazines has dispelled much of the mystery of working with an interior decorator. Every home owner, no matter how modest a residence or budget, has access to the time-saving help of a professional decorator. Because an interior decorator has wholesale resources and is experienced in all aspects of specifying quantities and sources, it is often much less expensive to work with an interior decorator rather than trying to do everything on your own.

A professional decorator is a facilitator and will keep you on track, guide random ideas, stimulate discussion, ask thought-provoking questions, and offer suggestions. The mission of an interior decorator is to guide each client's ideas to the most direct and pleasing conclusion.

Look for an interior decorator by previewing his/her work at home shows and design seminars, through ads in newspapers, magazines, and the yellow pages, and by recommendations from friends.

During the initial phone conversation, establish where the first meeting will take place and if there is a charge for the consultation. The most effective appointments take place in the client's home and should be complimentary.

In order to judge the scope of the project, the decorator needs to see your design challenge firsthand, and you deserve the opportunity to interview a decorator without being charged a fee.

ABOVE: Home decorating has become big business, and there are countless sources for every project you want to undertake. You may decide to hire an interior decorator to help you navigate your course. Gather as much information as you can during the early stages of your planning. It will help you know what questions to ask, and be able to judge whether pricing is competitive.

Keys to a Successful First Meeting

When meeting the decorator for the first time, there are some things you will want to keep in mind so that you don't waste time and money by being unprepared.

COMMUNICATION: Rapport and communication are essential to a successful client/decorator relationship. In the best of situations, these elements are established on the initial telephone call, and afterward, reinforced on the first house visit. A smart decorator will never make you feel ill at ease about the existing condition of your residence, or demand that you start from scratch. You should feel comfortable confiding your needs, wants, and dreams. In turn he/she is responsible to listen, interpret, and guide you to the most fitting solutions.

PHOTOGRAPHS: Cliché, but true—a picture is worth a thousand words. Prior to meeting with the decorator, collect pictures of rooms, colors, and treatments you both like and dislike. Ask the decorator to show you a portfolio of his/her work.

BUDGET: Be honest about your budget. A responsible decorator can provide you with beautiful results even when funds are limited. Decorating is a work-in-progress and often requires having a long-range plan.

THE SCOPE OF SERVICE: Determine if the decorator can do more than simply supply you with ideas. The best interior decorating services will take a project from concept to selection, and from ordering to installation. The decorator should be prepared to provide you with a contract showing the scope of services and their cost.

First-time Tip

The best referral for an interior decorator is their work and a happy previous client. Find a way to visit homes you admire. If they worked with a decorator, find out who it is. Friends and acquaintances will be more than happy to share their good experiences, and even more willing to talk about bad ones!

Equipping Yourself

Like any new undertaking, beginning a decorating project requires a few basics tools. Because planning is one of the important aspects of making certain your project is a success, you'll need a few things to keep you organized, and a place to record your thoughts and the information you'll be gathering through each phase of the process. Give yourself permission to spend a little more money on these items so that they're fun and you'll enjoy the time when you use them.

CARRY BAG: Buy a carry bag. Make certain it's light, but large enough to fit everything you'll be carrying with you while you're looking through fabric samples, wallpaper books, or doing other errands. Long straps make it easy to swing over your shoulder. Be certain there's room for magazines and a decorating book or two.

SKETCH BOOK: An artist's sketch book is a great place to store the dimensions of rooms, windows, etc. It gives you a place to do calculations and make notes. For fun, embellish the cover with some whimsical cutouts.

BLANK BOOK OR JOURNAL: You'll be recording your thoughts, likes, and dislikes in this book, so be certain there are plenty of pages in it. We'll be referring to this as your Decorating Journal throughout the book.

BINDER: A three-ring binder with dividers and sheet protectors is where you'll want to keep magazine articles you have clipped, brochures, paint samples, and fabric swatches. Create a section for each room you're working on.

TAPE MEASURE: An essential item, a purse-sized tape measure is lightweight and good for the types of things you'll be checking when you are out shopping.

CAMERA: A digital camera is perfect for decorating projects because you can download and print photos quickly for your notebook. Regardless of its type, keep a camera with you at all times to take photos of rooms you like—you're going to want to remember.

SCISSORS, TAPE, AND SMALL STAPLER: Art supply stores and specialty office supply retailers carry small versions of each of these tools. They will help keep you organized on the go.

First-time Tip

Purchase a color fan deck at a retail paint store, and carry it with your planning tools. You'll find it handy not only for choosing paint colors but also for matching fabrics and coordinating accessories. If you keep everything together in the carry bag, they'll be at hand when you need them. Consider keeping the bag in your car.

Working Tools

Gone are the days when tools were relegated to a man's tool bench. There are some basic tools that every decorator, man or woman, should not be without, and most of them are essential to each aspect of home decorating.

CORDLESS DRILL/SCREWDRIVER: Most cordless drills come with two batteries so you can always keep one charged. Be certain to keep an assortment of drill and screwdriver bits on hand.

ELECTRIC STAPLE GUN: You'll find this tool is good for upholstery projects and to make quick repairs to a variety of decorating projects.

BUILDER'S TAPE MEASURE: Be certain it is at least 50' long.

STURDY HAMMER: You want it to be strong enough to pull out stubborn nails, but not so heavy it's hard to hold when using it for other tasks.

PLIERS: Several styles including a needle-nosed pair is a good idea. Be certain one pair has a wire cutter.

(CLOCKWISE FROM TOP) A basic tool kit for a decorator should include a hammer, clamp, scissors, several types of pliers, a cutting blade, quake putty, an electric staple gun, a level, molly bolts, a multibit screwdriver, and a cordless drill/screwdriver.

CLAMPS: The newer plastic clamps will close tightly around many objects to give you an extra pair of hands. Be certain to choose clamps with a quick-release feature—they are much easier to use.

LEVEL: For heavy-duty jobs, you'll want a large level; but for hanging pictures, a small one works well.

MULTIPURPOSE MANUAL SCREWDRIVER: Look for a model that holds multiple bits that fit into the handle. This way you won't be looking for a new screwdriver every time you come across a different screw.

MOLLY BOLTS: A molly bolt (or wall anchor) goes into the wall to hold a screw securely in place. It is essential with drywall and sheetrock construction to use a molly bolt when hanging pictures, shelves, or other items on a wall. Without an anchor, the nail will pull out of the wall.

SCISSORS: Invest in a good sturdy pair.

TOP-QUALITY CUTTING BLADE: Buy one with a retractable safety feature.

QUAKE PUTTY: This has countless uses, including helping to keep pictures straight and marking walls when measuring where to put nail holes. The putty easily comes off the wall without a trace.

There is an assortment of tool boxes and kits on the market. Choose one that works for you and keep all of these essential tools in it. It's much easier to pick up the group of tools at once and carry it to where you are working than trying to track down each item as you work.

Style

Many decorating experts advise that it is imperative to define your decorating style before you start a project. They are right, but so much emphasis has been placed on choosing a style that it has become intimidating. The truth is that most people enjoy a blend of several different styles, which are constantly evolving. Stay open-minded and take time to go through an evaluation process.

Deciding what decorating style you prefer is a little like going into therapy. This is where your decorating journal comes in. Take time to sit quietly and record the answers to some very basic and meaningful questions. Ask yourself:

"Who am I?"

"How do I see myself?"

"How do I want others to see me?"

"What do I like?"

"When I spend time at home, what do I want to be doing?"

"How do I want to feel when I am at home?"

"Do I like to entertain?"

"Will I be having overnight guests?"

"Where do I see myself living in the next five to 10 years?"

ABOVE RIGHT: Gathering baskets and a classic fruit-print fabric make this room a sophisticated twist of Americana.

ABOVE LEFT: The use of pinks and greens and vintage-style lace makes this room romantic and reminiscent of a bygone era.

OPPOSITE PAGE TOP: Simple lines, muted color and stream-lined accessories give this room a comfortable urban chic style.

OPPOSITE PAGE BOTTOM: Depending on the fabric, a slip-cover can be formal or casual. In this girl's room, the chair is covered in white silk embellished with small seed-pearl beading to set a glamorous tone inspired by "Breakfast at Tiffany's."

Decorating Style Groups

Spend time perusing magazines and books to collect photos of rooms you like. You'll find yourself gravitating toward certain elements. Take note of what they are, and record them in your decorating journal.

Read back over what you've written and sort through the pictures you have clipped. Now you are ready to define your style. First, let's review the basic style groups.

CASUAL: Casual style usually has simple details, textured elements, and lots of horizontal lines. Furniture tends to be large scale and upholstered or slipcovered. Finishes are low luster or appear aged.

FORMAL: Formal style is inspired by period homes with elaborate architectural features. Symmetry and lines play a strong role in how furniture and accessories are arranged. Woods are high luster and gold-leaf finish is common in accessories.

CONTEMPORARY: Clean lines, sculptural furnishings, neutral elements, art, and bold decor define contemporary style.

TRADITIONAL: Comforting and classic, traditional style is similar to formal style, but it differs in that rooms are less grand and more relaxed. Often less-expensive furniture or reproductions are used and details are less fussy.

Now let's look at the myriad of styles that fall under each of the main categories.

ARCHITECTURAL: *Inspired by architectural styles:* Bungalow, Colonial, Cottage, Craftsman, Farmhouse, Georgian, Mission, Plantation, Tudor, or Victorian.

AROUND THE WORLD: *Inspired by places:* African, Asian, English Country, French Country, French Provincial, Paris Flea Market, Mediterranean, Tuscan, Moroccan, Mexican, Spanish, or Swedish.

GEOGRAPHY: *Inspired by locale:* Beach, Island/Tropical, Lakeside, Mountain, Sante Fe, Southwestern, or Western.

LIFESTYLE: *Inspired by hobbies or interests:* Eclectic, Elegant, Flea Market, Hi-Tech, Sports, Rustic, Resort, Urban Chic, or Whimsical.

Decorating Style Word Game

Take a few minutes to play a word game that will help define your own style. Using the styles above, put category words together to describe your look. Here are a few examples:

> rustic-elegance
>
> beach-bungalow
>
> casual-whimsical

Allow yourself to mix and match until you feel you have described your style. Record your answers in your decorating journal. Finally, take some time to write down your vision of the room you are working on. What does the furniture look like? What type of window covering is there? What type is the floor covering? Can you see a wall color? If you can't answer any of these questions yet, don't worry—it's a process, and you are well on your way.

LEFT: This room has elements of Mediterranean and Tuscan styles and is given personality with the brightly hued contemporary artwork on the wall.

ABOVE: This room is an array of vibrant color, yet it is softened by the light green walls. The muted walls are a perfect companion to the jewel-toned fabric and accessory pillows.

Color

Color can be a great source of passion and excitement, yet first-time decorators are afraid of it. Sometimes it isn't so much that we are afraid of what to choose, it's that we like so many colors. The attraction to many colors at the same time can create a palette paralysis—you just aren't sure where to start. Color selection extends beyond walls to flooring, fabrics, window treatments, and accessories.

If you've established the parameters of your personal decorating style, you are well on your way to choosing colors that will work for you. Certain styles naturally lend themselves to specific colors. With style as your guide, you should have some feel for your first choice of color. First, it's important to review a few principles of color.

THE IVES COLOR WHEEL: The Ives Color Wheel is used in printmaking, dying, photography, and other arts. The basic color wheel is just three colors: yellow, magenta, and cyan (blue). The wheel is stepped out into 12, 24, and 48 color sections, depending on how detailed the use of color is going to be. For the sake of discussing basic color, we'll look at the 24-step wheel. Each step represents the pure form of a particular color. Each pure color has hues, tints, and shades. The degree in which different amounts of each color is mixed and blended is what creates the beautiful colors we see in home decor today. Keep the color wheel in mind as we review five approaches to working with color.

FIVE BASIC COLOR PLANS:

Monochromatic: Select one color and use only its tints, shades, and tones. An example is choosing to paint and decorate an entire room in shades of taupe.

Complementary: Select two colors that are opposite each other on the color wheel. Yellow and blue are opposite each other on the wheel and are a classic pair in home decorating.

Analogous: Choose a color on the wheel, then choose one, two, or three neighboring colors on either side of it on the wheel.

Split Complementary: This combines analogous and complementary schemes. Choose one color and its complementary color. Now, choose several analogous colors to the complementary color. You can use either your first-choice color or the complementary as the dominant color in your scheme.

Triadic: Select a favorite color. Then, dividing the color wheel in thirds, choose the two colors that are equal distance from each other on the wheel.

Monochromatic

Analogous

Split Complementary

Triadic

Understanding these basics will demystify the selection process and may make it easier for you to experiment with colors you think you'd like to use.

Invest in a paint color deck, sometimes called a fan deck. You can purchase one at your local paint retailer. It's a great resource for experimenting and choosing colors.

Paint sample cards, referred to as paint chips, work well for mixing and matching colors when you're trying to make decisions. Once you decide on your scheme, get several samples of each color to put in your notebook. You will find yourself referring to them often.

ABOVE AND OPPOSITE PAGE: Don't be afraid to mix colors on adjoining walls. Stay within the same color tones. If you choose a bright color for one wall, use equally bright shades or a neutral tone for the adjoining areas. While pastels may be very different, soft tones pull the different colors together.

Fabric

Fabrics bring color, texture, and depth to a room. One of the best assets of patterned and print fabrics is that experienced designers and artists already have worked to blend complementary or contrasting colors for you. The hard work is done; you just have to choose the fabrics you like and that suit your lifestyle. Before you get serious about your choices, there are a few things to think about.

What is the room's exposure to sunlight? Warm colors are suited for northern- and eastern-facing rooms, while western- and southern-facing rooms do better with cool color schemes. You'll also want to take note how much full sunlight the fabrics will be exposed to and be certain to choose a fabric that is fade resistant.

Do you want to increase or decrease how the room seems? Warm colors make a room seem smaller; cool colors make a room feel larger.

How much wear will the fabric have to withstand? Delicate fabrics are not good choices for upholstered furniture, and likewise, heavy fabrics are not suitable for curtains or drapes.

TOP: This girl's room is a showcase of fabric. Generous amounts of fabric are used for the swags and jabots on the windows.

ABOVE: The floral pattern on the bedding complements the plaid drapery fabric

Mixing It Up

If you are going to work with anything other than a monochromatic palette, start by choosing a print you love. This is considered your "signature print" and will set the theme for your room. It's best if it contains several colors and a large-scale pattern suitable for window treatments, bed coverings, wall coverings, and upholstered furniture.

Choose one color from the signature print to be the dominant coordinate. Then, pull two or three other colors for accent colors. Use these in pillows, welting, inverted pleats, or other details. Avoid using the same patterns, such as two florals. Use a floral and a stripe instead.

If you use varying versions of the color scheme throughout the house, you'll find it easy to pull together furniture.

TOP: The texture and woven detail of the fabric on the chair and ottoman bring this room to life.

ABOVE: Choose one fabric as the "signature," then choose another pattern to be the main complement, filling in with accent colors.

Flooring

How you choose to cover your floors is a decision you will be reminded of every time you walk into your home. Whether you decide on carpet for comfort, wood for aesthetics, tile for durability, or laminate for budget—you'll walk on it for years to come.

Carpet

Carpet adds warmth and quiet to a home like no other floor covering. Its softness insulates against cold and absorbs sound. Carpet can also absorb many things you don't want it to, such as spilled drinks and pet stains; so depending on your lifestyle, it may be best used in bedrooms, living rooms, and other low-traffic areas.

New technology has made a variety of textured carpets affordable. Textures, colors, and pattern can incorporate diamonds, bows, pin dots, or flowers in sculptural effects. The cost of carpet is based on fiber, construction, and quality. Adding to the expense is quality carpet padding and installation. Before you shop for carpet, familiarize yourself with the following terms:

Measure Up

Determining how much carpet you'll need can be tricky. Be certain to have your retailer do the final measurement for you. However, when you're planning and budgeting, you'll want to have some idea of the quantity needed.

Begin by multiplying the length of the room by its width (feet) for the square footage. To get the square yardage, divide by nine. Your retailer will know how to measure to include hallways and closets, match patterns and plan seam placement. All of these factors will increase the square footage or yardage you will need.

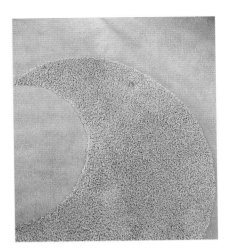

TOP: A creative way to blend one type of carpet into another used in a different room is to make the transition with a geometric or whimsical design. This transition is coming off the top stair of a landing into a game room.

ABOVE: Different patterned and textured carpets can be used in different rooms—just be sure to use natural room breaks such as doorways, top stair, and room step-ups as the defining line. This combination works because the color tones are similar.

CUT PILE: Loops are cut, leaving individual yarn tufts. Its durability depends on the type of fiber, density of tufts, and the amount of twist in the yarn. Density is the amount of pile yarn in the carpet—the denser, the better. Twist is the winding of the yarn around itself.

PLUSH/VELVET: Smooth level surfaces; formal atmosphere, "velvet."

SAXONY: Smooth level finish, but pile yarns have more twist so the yarn ends are visible and create a less formal look. This carpet minimizes footprints.

FRIEZE: Yarns are extremely twisted, forming a "curly" textured surface. This informal look also minimizes footprints and vacuum marks.

LEVEL-LOOP PILE: Loops are the same height, creating an informal look. It generally lasts a long time in high-traffic areas. Many of today's popular Berber styles are level-loop styles with flecks of a darker color on a lighter background.

MULTILEVEL LOOP: Usually has two to three different loop heights to create pattern effects, providing good durability and a more casual look.

CUT-AND-LOOP PILE: Combination of cut and looped yarns that provides a variety of surface textures, including sculptured effects of squares, chevrons, swirls, etc.

Fibers

Fiber is carpet's basic ingredient. The type of fiber used and the way the carpet is constructed determine how well the carpet will stand up to spills, pets, and daily traffic. Approximately 97 percent of all carpet is produced using synthetic fibers designed to feature style, easy maintenance, and outstanding value. There are five basic types of carpet pile fibers.

NYLON: Wear-resistant, resilient, withstands the weight and movement of furniture and provides brilliant color. Known for its ability to conceal and resist soils and stains, it is generally good for all traffic areas. Solution-dyed nylon is colorfast because color is added in the fiber production.

OLEFIN (POLYPROPYLENE): Strong, resists wear and permanent stains, is easily cleaned, and notably colorfast because color is added during the fiber production. Resists static electricity and is often used in both indoor and outdoor installations because of its resistance to moisture and mildew. Many Berbers are made of olefin.

POLYESTER: Noted for luxurious, soft "hand" when used in thick cut-pile textures and has excellent color clarity and retention. It's easily cleaned, and resistant to water-soluble stains.

ACYRLIC: Offers the appearance and feel of wool without the cost, has low static level, and is moisture- and mildew-resistant. Commonly used in velvet and level-loop constructions, and often in bath and scatter rugs.

WOOL: Noted for its luxury and performance, wool is soft, has high bulk, and is available in many colors. Generally, wool is somewhat more expensive than synthetic fibers.

BLENDS: A wool/nylon blend combines the superior look and comfort of wool with the durability of nylon. Acrylic/olefin and nylon/olefin are other popular blends, offering good characteristics of each fiber.

ABOVE: Wood floors that are specially designed to look worn add style to decor and are very durable because they don't show wear.

Wood

A wood floor is a good choice for beauty and durability. Whether you are buying a new wood floor or refinishing an old one, you need to be familiar with the different types of wood floors. Be certain to research the moisture content of your foundation if you're laying wood over a concrete slab. A moisture barrier is imperative, and the slab should be sealed thoroughly before the wood floor is installed.

SOLID WOOD: Made of hardwood, can be installed on a concrete slab or directly on a subfloor. A good hardwood floor expands and contracts with a home's humidity and can be sanded and refinished several times over its life. Hardwood is graded for color, grain, and pattern, which is determined by the species of the tree the wood comes from and what part of the log it is cut from.

STRIP FLOORING: Generally strips are 2" wide, but they can range from 1"–3", and are installed by nailing to the subfloor.

PLANK FLOORING BOARDS: At least 3"-wide, they can be screwed or nailed to the subfloor. Screw holes are covered with plugs.

PARQUET FLOORING: Comes in standard patterns of 6" square blocks. Specialty patterns may range up to 36"-square units. Parquet often achieves dramatic effects in geometric design patterns.

First-time Tip

If you have inherited a worn wood floor and you would rather put your money into other parts of your decorating budget for now, consider painting or stenciling the floor. Painted wood floors can be very attractive and are a quick way to brighten a room.

ABOVE: Wood's rich beauty and resistance to liquid spills makes it an excellent choice for main living areas such as dining rooms and living rooms. Solid wood flooring can withstand years of wear and can be refinished several times over the life of a house.

ENGINEERED WOOD: Made from several layers of different woods or grades of the same wood stacked and glued together under heat and pressure. Some engineered-wood floors with thick top layers can be sanded many times.

WOOD LAMINATES: Made using a plywood base topped with a layer of veneer. Plies and thickness vary, but three-ply, $3/8$" flooring is most common. The veneer topping of wood-laminate floors can be sanded and refinished about three times.

Other Surfaces

There are quite a few options when it comes to flooring. If you want to stay clear of carpet and wood, here are some other options.

CERAMIC TILE AND NATURAL STONE: Both tile and natural stone floors are beautiful and will last the lifetime of a house. Chances are you will not be investing in natural stone for a first-time decorating project. Yet, with so many advances in tile flooring, it is possible to get the same look with tile.

Tile floors are a great choice for high-traffic areas and families with children and pets. The patterns and designs available by mixing tiles can make a floor a work of art that is fairly easy to maintain. Ceramic floor tiles are either glazed or unglazed. Unglazed tiles include quarry tiles, encaustic (a paint made from pigment mixed with melted beeswax and resin and after application, fixed by heat), geometric tiles, and ceramic mosaic tiles, which can be either glazed or unglazed. Most other ceramic floor tiles are glazed.

LAMINATES: Laminate flooring has four main components that are bonded together. A wear-resistant decorative surface made of resin-based melamine/aluminum oxide is bonded to a wood-composition core. A backing is bonded to the underside of the core, and on the decorative surface is a sheet of aluminum oxide to provide protection and stain resistance. The surface contains a photographic image of whatever the laminate is imitating: wood, stone, or marble. Most laminates are installed in a tongue-and-groove system and can be set over existing flooring. Laminate floors are either installed in planks or squares.

VINYL AND LINOLEUM: Linoleum and vinyl flooring, like everything else, has come a long way the last few years. These floors are good for playrooms and children's rooms, and are a great choice if you want to save money now and plan to replace the floor in a few years. They are resilient and because of the slight cushion in the construction, these floors can be quieter and more comfortable to walk on than other floors.

Vinyl and linoleum floors can be laid in sheets or are available in tiles, allowing for flexibility with pattern and color variations.

TOP FAR LEFT: Mosaic borders incorporated into tile designs using larger pieces make interesting floor patterns.

TOP CENTER LEFT: A circular mosaic set into a wood floor in an entry makes a dramatic "rug" that withstands heavy traffic and is easily cleaned.

TOP CENTER RIGHT: By staggering floor tiles slightly and incorporating small accent tiles into the pattern, this floor becomes stylish and sophisticated.

TOP FAR RIGHT: Vinyl "tiles" resembling stone come with a faux grout border. When the tiles are installed, it's difficult to tell the floor is not ceramic.

ABOVE: Home improvement stores carry many options of pre-spaced floor tiles. Rather than having to painstakingly lay tile, these sections can be purchased and trimmed to fit a specific space. Once the tiles are in place, apply grout, clean, and let dry.

OPPOSITE PAGE: The true beauty of natural stone is showcased in a geometric design.

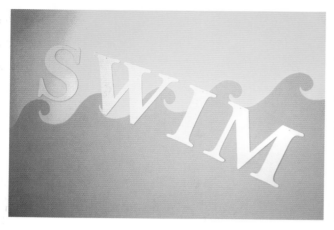

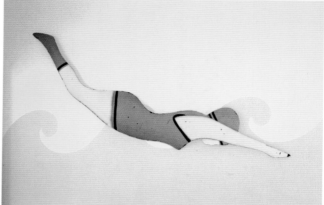

Walls

Walls are the canvas against which your decorating efforts will be showcased. They define the feeling of a room, whether you choose paint, faux finishing, paneling, stonework, or wallpaper. While each of these has its own distinct style and advantage, first-time decorators generally choose paint or wallpaper because of budget and the fact that these two treatments can be simple do-it-yourself projects.

Paint

Paint is available in either latex (water based) or enamel (oil based). Because it's easier to apply and clean up, it is advisable to use water-based paint. Paint is available in five different sheens. The shinier the finish, the more durable the paint.

HIGH GLOSS: The shiniest: washable, durable, and used on accent surfaces like wood trim.

SEMIGLOSS: Less shiny, but just as durable and washable.

PEARL/SATIN: Has a slight shine and is washable.

EGGSHELL: Used if no shine is desired. Good for imperfect walls. Washable.

FLAT: Commonly used, but is not nearly as durable or washable as the other sheens. If you need to wash a wall, you'll have to wash the entire surface.

First-time Tip

You'll never know for sure how a paint color will look until you try it in the room you are planning to paint. Buy a quart of several colors you are seriously considering and paint each on one large square of white mat board. Lean boards against the walls. If you paint directly on the wall, it is often difficult to cover up with selected paint color. Look at the colors at different times of the day in various lighting. You may find that what looked so good on a paint chip is a disaster at home.

ABOVE: This kitchen in a newly constructed house was once cold and stark. Soft yellow walls, with a hand-painted motif of vines, give the space a warm feel. The budget for the paint, window coverings, area rug, and accessories was less than $500.

RIGHT: Walls can be easily decorated with freehand brush strokes. Here, a large artist's watercolor brush and white paint were used to create a branch design on a sage green wall.

If you are personally going to undertake a painting job, abide by the advice of a professional painter—the prep time takes as long as the actual painting job itself. Be certain to tape off the area to ensure you paint only the surface you want, wash and sand walls for a smooth surface, and use the right brushes and rollers for the job.

Before you begin, take your wall measurements with you to the paint store. Your retailer will be able to tell you how much paint you'll need for your project.

The best thing about painting walls is that if you make a mistake—or don't like the color—you can paint right over your first attempt.

Wallpaper

Wallpaper is a wonderful way to use color and pattern on a wall without having to learn a faux-finish technique, and the selection of styles is endless. Listed are the most popular types of wallpaper you'll find at your local retailer or home improvement store.

VINYL-COATED PAPER: Has a paper base on which the decorative surface has been sprayed or coated with an acrylic-type vinyl or polyvinyl chloride (PVC). These wallpapers are scrubbable and strippable, and are suited for most areas. They are more resistant to grease and moisture than plain paper, and are good for bathrooms and kitchens.

COATED FABRIC: Has a fabric base, coated with liquid vinyl or acrylic. The decorative layer is printed on this coating. It's generally considered more "breathable" wallpaper, which makes it best for use in low-moisture rooms like living areas.

First-time Tip

When ordering wallpaper, always order at least one more roll than you will need. That way, if you ever need to repair or replace a section, you have paper from the same dye lot.

PAPER-BACKED VINYL/SOLID SHEET VINYL: Has a paper (pulp) base, laminated to a solid decorative surface. This type of wallpaper is very durable since the decorative surface is a solid sheet of vinyl. It's scrubbable and peelable. Solid sheet vinyl can be used in most areas of the home since it resists moisture and is stain and grease resistant. However, this type of wallpaper will not withstand hard physical abuse areas such as mudrooms or laundry rooms.

FABRIC-BACKED VINYL: Has a base laminated to a solid vinyl decorative surface. General categories of this type of wallpaper include:

SOLID VINYL: Consists of a vinyl film laminated to a fabric or paper base. It's more durable than fabric- or paper-backed vinyl because the vinyl is "solid" or not applied in a liquid form. This type of wallpaper is the most durable.

PAPER: This refers to wallpaper with a paper substrate/ground combination upon which the decorative layer is printed. True papers are not coated, but some may have a coating applied to seal in the inks. While this type of wallpaper can be delicate, it is generally very attractive.

Wallpaper comes in single- and double-roll quantities and in a variety of widths. You'll need to allow for pattern repeat and some waste. Your wallpaper retailer can help with the specifics of the particular wall covering you have chosen.

Measure Up

The most important step in estimating wall covering is accurate measurements. Use a yardstick or steel tape measure, never a cloth tape measure. Take measurements in feet, rounding off to the next highest half foot or foot. Draw a room diagram showing doors, windows, and ceiling height. If a wall is unusually broken up with a fireplace, built-in bookcases, etc., a diagram with detailed measurements is necessary in figuring square footage of wall covering needed.

Measure wall height from floor to ceiling. Exclude baseboards and moldings. Measure length of each wall including doors and windows. Find the total square feet of the wall(s) by multiplying ceiling height by total wall length. Subtract areas that will not be covered. (Standard doors are about 3' x 7', or 21' square; standard windows about 3' x 4', or 12' square.)

These calculations give the total number of square feet to be covered. Using this method, the number of rolls or linear yards of wall covering can be determined.

ABOVE: A hot trend in interior decor is to cover a wall or walls of a room with stone or brick. In this room, stone was installed on all four walls to make the room seem small and intimate.

RIGHT: Adding paneling is a classic way to dress a wall. In this bedroom the paneling was installed three-quarters of the way up the wall and appears to be the headboard for the bed.

ABOVE: Molding can be used to create many effects. In this room, wide molding is used on the wall around the bed to create a large frame. The inside of the frame is upholstered with batting and a designer fabric to create the look of a headboard. A thin strip molding is used to accent wall sconces. The room is finished with a crown molding.

Molding and Millwork

Decorative molding and millwork were once the domain of a skilled carpenter. Thanks to the innovations of urethane molding, most first-time decorators can install a wide variety of crown molding, chair rails, door trims, and other architectural accents. Miterless corner systems require only straight cuts. The corner piece is easily matched with the flat end of the molding to create a seamless trim that once took hours of painstaking work.

Other millwork that makes a great addition to a room are ceiling medallions, door surrounds, and window trim.

ABOVE: Many ornate moldings and decorative ornamentations are available in urethane which makes it easy to work with and contracts and expands with humidity and heat after it is installed.

LEFT: Miterless corner systems make installing crown molding simple. After the corner is installed, the length of molding is measured, cut, and installed in the space between the two corners.

Crown Molding

Look at an older home, whether a stately manor or a cozy cottage, and you're likely to find crown molding. Most builders omit this detail in new homes. If you are familiar with working with a saw and miter box, you will find crown molding easy to install. If not, it's a good idea to leave this job for a professional. You can save cost by painting the molding the color of your choice.

Installing Crown Molding

The following are instructions for installing crown molding with miterless corners.

1. Measure the length of the ceiling. Select the molding profile and inside and outside corners to be used. Subtract the size of the corners from the overall ceiling length.

2. For each 10' of space left after you subtract for the corners, add 1" to the overall length. This is the amount of molding you'll need for the ceiling space to ensure a tight fit, which is imperative because molding will expand and contract slightly with changes in temperature.

3. Install inside and outside corners to the walls first.

4. Use a top-quality urethane construction adhesive along the back of the corners and make certain to cover all joints with adhesive.

5. Firmly place the miterless corners into each corner of the wall near the ceiling. Wipe off any excess adhesive immediately.

6. Fasten corners in place with nails. Countersink the nails, and fill in with wood filler or caulking. Let it dry completely, then lightly sand the surface smooth.

7. Using a saw and a miter box, make straight cuts on your molding to fit your measurements.

8. Install molding the same way as the corners, securing with urethane adhesive, then nailing in place about every 16". These pieces should fit snugly against the corners.

9. On the molding, countersink nails, fill with wood filler or caulking, let dry, then lightly sand the area until smooth. Use a good-quality latex or oil-based paint on the molding and corners. No primer coat is needed.

Ceiling Medallions

Installing a ceiling medallion is a simple process. Most medallions on the market are made of preformed foam that can be painted whatever color you choose with any type of paint. The hanging light fixture must be removed from the ceiling chain in order to install the medallion.

ABOVE AND OPPOSITE PAGE: Once reserved for manor homes, ceiling medallions are enjoying a revival in popularity. Easily installed, they add a finishing touch to a hanging light fixture in a formal room or entry area.

Installing a Ceiling Medallion

Installing a ceiling medallion like the one at left is a simple way to embellish a room. There are only a few simple steps.

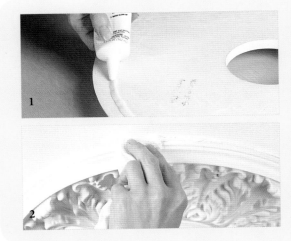

1. Place a generous amount of urethane construction adhesive around the perimeter and interior of the medallion. Let the adhesive begin to set, then position the medallion on the ceiling around the electrical opening from which the fixture hangs.

2. Hold the medallion in place for a few minutes until you are sure that the adhesive is secured to the ceiling. Once the adhesive has dried, hang the light fixture.

Windows

Y ou may tend to think of windows as a practical part of your home through which the sun illuminates your interior spaces. When used as part of interior decor, however, a window can be a glittering jewel in a decorating scheme. Innovative usage of windows—either inside or out— creates privacy and opens rooms up to light.

TOP: Using decorative leaded-glass windows in an entry is an elegant way to tie the out-doors and interior together.

ABOVE: If your budget doesn't allow for installing decorative windows, there are craft kits available that make it easy to get the same effect. The kits come with liquid leading or pre-formed designs. Glass finishes are achieved by using specific liquid compounds and following easy directions to create patterns.

LEFT: This bathroom shows two good uses of window materials. The double-hung, beveled-glass window attractively screens for privacy and is an updated alternative to the standard rain-glass bathroom window. The clear-glass-block windows in the shower wall allow dif-fused light to pass in from the room. Clear blocks are available in glass and acrylic and are installed inside a frame.

OPPOSITE PAGE: Rather than having a solid wall between the dining room and living room, beveled-glass windows allow light to pass between rooms while creating an elegant wall between both spaces. Less expensive than exte-rior windows, these windows add a dimension and air of elegance.

Window Coverings

There is so much to know about window coverings that an encyclopedia detailing each one has been written. Often the deciding factor in the choice of window coverings is personal taste. Some think that swags and jabots are the be all and end all, while others wouldn't be caught dead with that much fabric around a window.

One of the most commonly confused window-covering descriptions is the difference between drapery and curtains. Drapery is hung from a traverse rod, typically has pleated headings and oftentimes is lined. Curtains are considered more casual and are either hung from rings or a casing that a rod slips through.

ABOVE: Roman shades with a balloon-style bottom and finished with beaded trim are a tailored complement to this sunroom. Choosing shades that are installed inside the window frame keeps the attractive molding in full view.

OPPOSITE PAGE: A custom-made valance installed above drapery can make a room look finished and professionally decorated.

Useful Window Covering Terms

Here are a few basic terms you'll want to know before you shop for window coverings.

BALLOON SHADE: A shade made with vertical rows of horizontally gathered fabric that can be drawn up to form folded or pleated layers.

BLIND: A hard treatment of narrow strips made from plastic, metal, or wood that raises with a pulley system.

CENTER DRAW: When a pair of draperies open and close exactly at a window's center point.

CORNICE: A shallow (usually wood) box atop a window to hide drapery or curtain hardware.

DRESS CURTAINS: Stationary curtains meant for decorative purposes only.

FESTOON: Decorative drapery made of folded fabric that hangs in graceful curves, framing the top of a window.

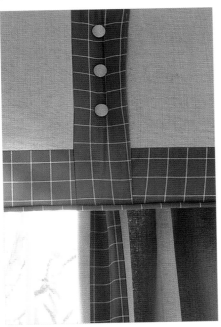

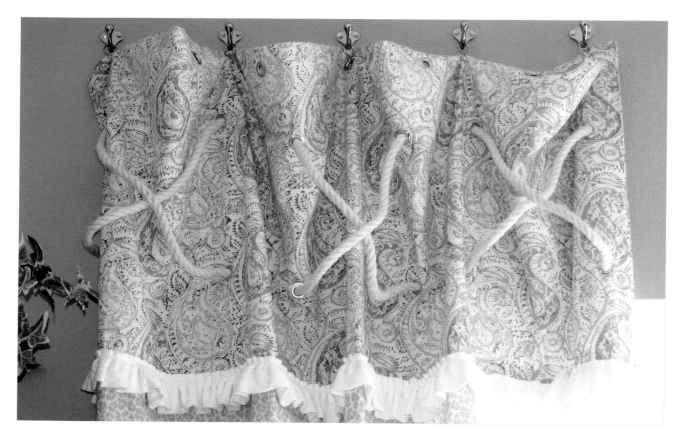

FLOUNCE: An extra-long heading sewn at the top of a rod pocket that falls over the rod to create the appearance of an attached valance.

JABOT: A decorative vertical end of an overtreatment usually finished in a horizontal festoon.

LAMBREQUIN: A fabric cornice that completely frames the top of a window.

ONE-WAY DRAW: Drapery designed to draw one panel in one direction.

PASSEMENTERIE (pronounced "pass-a-mint-terry"): Trimmings and decorative edges.

ROLLER SHADE: A horizontal shade operated by a spring device.

ROMAN SHADE: A corded shade with rods set horizontally in back to give it a number of neat folds when raised.

SHIRRING: When a rod shorter than the fabric width is slid through a rod pocket to create a gathered curtain or valance.

TRAVERSE ROD: A rod operated by a cord and pulley.

VALANCE: A horizontal fabric treatment installed at the top of draperies to hide hardware and cords.

TOP: Metal utility hooks attached to the wall hold a casual flounce valance.

ABOVE: A sporty valance is suspended from skateboard wheels affixed to the wall in a boy's room.

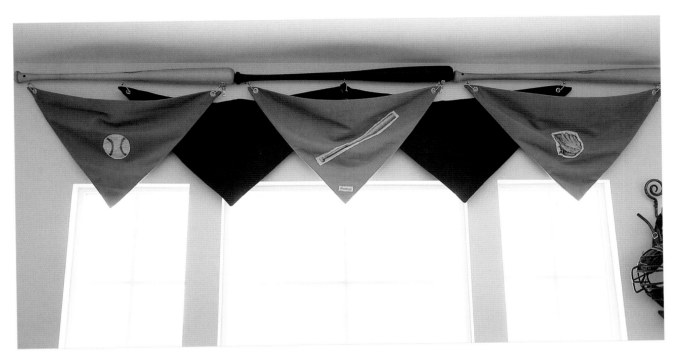

A little sewing savvy goes a long way in making a window valance. A valance is generally suspended from a rod or hooks, while a cornice is attached to a wood (cornice) box and attached to the wall with brackets. Consider purchasing premade valances and embellishing them with trims, appliqués, or other adornments.

TOP: Baseball bats are called off the field and placed above a window to hold this valance.

ABOVE: After this easy valance was sewn, silk flowers were attached and the valance was clipped to rod rings and mounted on a rod above the window.

Window treatments define the personality of a room. A shade or blind may block light and provide privacy; but add trim or scalloped edge, and it goes from practical to elegant or whimsical instantly. The same goes for curtains and drapery. If you decide that keeping light or the neighbors out is not necessary, a stationery jabot or window scarf may suffice. When choosing fabrics, be certain to consider the strong sunlight it will be exposed to. It can be heartbreaking to spend money and effort on a window treatment you adore, and find it deteriorating a year or two later.

ABOVE: While tailored window coverings have their place, you can achieve wonderful style with a more casual approach—loosely wrapping fabric and sheers around a rod or long branch.

OPPOSITE PAGE TOP LEFT AND RIGHT: Beaded trims add sparkle to window treatments. These details show that special thought was put into the design of shades and valances.

It doesn't take much sewing know-how to make window coverings. Often you can buy window coverings and simply embellish them. With a good pattern and/or measurements, you can sew swags like that shown above. The look of designer drapery can be easily achieved by buying a set of store-bought drapes and adding large sections of contrasting fabric, as shown at far left. All that's required is some quick measurements and straight lines sewn with a sewing machine.

TOP LEFT: Molding gives a ceiling dimension. If you are adding architectural elements like this after construction of the home, the molding and faux beams are a great way to hide new electrical conduits for lighting or sound systems.

TOP RIGHT: To create a mural on the ceiling of this study, the designer enlarged an Old World map and glued it to the ceiling. Spackle was sparingly applied to sections of the ceiling to make it look aged. The ceiling was then stained and glazed. The overall look gives the appearance of the ceiling having crumbled away, exposing an old map.

LEFT: Once relegated to sterile Victorian kitchens, metal ceilings are a decorative option that may be enjoyed in any room of the house.

OPPOSITE PAGE: Wood and beam ceilings are reminiscent of mountain retreats and make even an urban room feel cozy.

Ceilings

Ceilings, often referred to by designers as the fifth wall, should not be ignored. An embellished ceiling adds dimension to a room and makes it complete. Decorating a ceiling can be as simple as painting it a coordinating or contrasting color to the rest of the room. A ceiling can become ornate by adding custom molding or stenciling a mural. Whichever you choose, be sure not to skip the room's crowning glory.

Lighting

When residential builders are working on new homes, the lighting is planned long before anyone has thought about paint color or fabric swatches. You'd be wise to take heed! Bad lighting can make a room look dreadful and make it very difficult to work, read, or relax. There are three major categories of lighting to consider.

GENERAL LIGHTING: Provides overall illumination, and is also called ambient lighting. It radiates a comfortable level of brightness. Chandeliers, ceiling- or wall-mounted fixtures, and recessed or track lighting are all general lighting.

TASK LIGHTING: Helps light specific tasks such as cooking, reading, sewing, or desk work. Task lighting can be fluorescent lights installed under kitchen cabinets, hanging pendant lights, or portable lamps.

DECORATIVE LIGHTING: Adds drama to a room by creating visual interest. Also known as accent lighting, it can be a fixture that is part of a decorating scheme or a spotlight on paintings or plants.

A dimmer switch can work wonders to instantly change the mood in a room. Consider having dimmer switches on all lighting.

OPPOSITE PAGE: This kitchen shows the three basic lighting types. The recessed cans in the ceiling are general lighting, the lights under the cabinets are task lighting and the hanging pendant lights are decorative. The pendants can also act as task lighting, but the design of the fixture also adds to the decor.

BELOW: Natural light is the truest and most beautiful light and should not be ignored when decorating a room. Pay attention to the orientation of the room to the sun, and place furniture where it can best be enjoyed. The sun streaming through the windows of this home make it an obvious choice to place two comfortable sofas in front of the windows to optimize the beautiful natural light.

How High Is High? How Low Is Low?

Choosing a hanging fixture and deciding what height it should be a can pose a challenge if you don't follow a few guidelines. Residential lighting expert Deanne Carey offers these tips:

DINING ROOMS: One of the mistakes people make is thinking that a large room equates to a large hanging fixture. The width of the dining table determines the size of the fixture. If you doubt her, imagine a 56" round fixture

ABOVE: Pendant lights over the eating peninsula ensure there will be plenty of light for whatever tasks someone chooses to do while sitting there. There are no fluorescent lights in this kitchen; general light is provided by recessed can lights.

OPPOSITE PAGE: The width of the dining table determines the size of the fixture that hangs above it.

over a 48"-wide table. Guests will hit their head when pushing back from the table and standing. The fixture should not be smaller than the width of the table, and should not be more than two-thirds its width. Dining room fixtures should hang five feet off the ground.

ENTRIES: When deciding on size for an entry fixture, first measure from the ceiling down to 6" above the top of the entry door. The fixture should hang 6"–18" higher than the top of the door. The fixture should not be larger than one-third of this measurement.

Measure Up

To determine the size of an entry fixture, measure from the ceiling to 6" above the clearance of the entry door. Your fixture should be approximately one-third of this measurement.

Furniture

The saying, "You get what you pay for," is never truer than when it comes to the purchase of furniture. Furniture is the most important decorating investment you are going to make. A good piece of furniture will go with you wherever you may move in the years to come. You'll recoup your investment many times over if you invest now in good-quality pieces.

Upholstered Furniture

Materials and construction are very important. The obvious—and first—thing to consider is the fabric. Take a good look at it. The longest-lasting fabrics are made of closely woven strong fibers. Check the fabric carefully, remembering that a fabric is only as strong as its weakest fiber. What looks lovely may not wear well.

Next, consider the tailoring. Check the seams, stitching, details, and construction. If fabrics with patterns or plaids don't match up at the seams, it's a pretty good bet that the piece is not well made under the upholstery either.

The frame of the piece should be wood, well padded, and smooth. Watch out for frames that are built up with foam, paper, and other subquality materials.

Springs should be securely attached at the base of the frame and proportionately spaced. The highest quality upholstered pieces have eight-way hand-tied springs.

Quality pieces are stuffed with down. If polyurethane foam is used, be certain it is over 1.8 pounds per cubic foot. The foam will break down over time, while the down will be comfortable for decades.

ABOVE: A chair that mixes over-stuffed upholstered comfort with sleek wooden arms brings vintage and contemporary style together.

OPPOSITE PAGE: The wooden bed frame, upholstered chairs, and woven table blend together to create a comfortable contemporary room.

BELOW: Tufted upholstered chairs and an ottoman arranged facing each other create a cozy corner for reading or conversation.

Wood Furniture

Solid hardwood is the best quality of wood used in furniture construction. Less-expensive furniture is made with veneer, a decorative wood adhered to plywood, particle board, or other inexpensive wood grades. Budget furniture is often constructed from fiberboard covered with paper printed with a photographic copy of real wood. You'll find that this type of furniture is short-lived.

Dressers, chests, and armoires are sometimes referred to in the furniture industry as case goods. Good-quality case goods have dovetailed joints, meaning they are notched to interface at the joint rather than glued together. Pull out a drawer and look at how the edges are joined. Quality drawers sit evenly and have a good slider system with dust panels between each drawer so you can't see down into the drawer below. Look for the manufacturer's name stamped on the side of the upper-left drawer of the piece.

When shopping for chairs and tables, be certain that joint construction is sturdy. The legs should be firmly secured, and chair seats joined at the frame. Nothing should wobble.

With all-wood construction, check that grains match and are going in the same direction. Finishes should be hand-rubbed.

Leather

Leather is more durable than fabric if it is treated properly. Be certain you purchase full-grained leather, which is the best quality. Corrected grain leather has simply been machine stamped with a grain. It is not strong and will not withstand wear. Stay away from "splits," which means the leather is mixed with other parts of the hide including the fatty tissue that is compressed and mixed with the other grades of leather. Check out the underside of the piece to be certain that the leather is dyed all the way through. If you see a vinyl or fabric backing, it's not leather.

ABOVE: Quality wood furniture is destined to become an heirloom. When you budget for furniture purchases, take into consideration that by spending more on quality furniture, you'll never have to incur the expense again. Budget furniture will have to be replaced within a few years.

LEFT: Leather does not have to be relegated to chairs and sofas. Its durability and resistance to spills makes it a good material for ottomans and foot stools. This large leather ottoman serves as a table and brings a masculine tone to the room.

Metal Furniture

Metal furniture should be solidly constructed. Avoid hollow pieces—they dent easily and do not wear well. Be certain the finish is baked on. Iron pieces should be treated with an antirust finish. Check all welding joints. If it is good quality, all joints will be well constructed and you will not see any drips of metal.

Woven Furniture

Woven furniture may be made from a number of different materials. Most wicker is made from either natural reed or paper fiber. Rattan is a natural material imported from China, Southeast Asia, Malaysia, and the Philippines that resembles grapevine.

Bamboo resembles rattan and is often mistaken for it. One of the biggest differences between the two materials is that bamboo has a hollow core center and rattan has a solid core center. Bamboo tends to split and break more easily than rattan.

Paper-fiber rush wicker is a man-made paper product invented in 1904, and resembles rope or cord. It can be durable if it is tightly wound and the finished piece is well painted and sealed. It is not suitable for outdoors.

TOP: If you are going for a casually elegant look, wood and iron make a good combination for a coffee table.

ABOVE: The texture and coloring of natural woven furniture brings a relaxing resort style to a room. Look for strong rattan material or quality wicker when shopping for woven furniture.

Slipcovered Furniture

Slipcovered furniture has made a comeback in recent years, and for good reason. Slipcovers provide many decorating alternatives as they can be changed with the seasons to give the same piece of furniture a completely different look.

Depending on the fabric, a slipcover can be formal or casual. Slipcovers can be purchased at most department stores, or can be homemade. Most sewing machine Web sites have instructions for simple slipcovers.

ABOVE LEFT: This slipcovered table is an innovative idea. The base is covered with a tailored fabric skirt and topped with wood. The same look can be achieved by using a wooden serving tray atop an inexpensive base. A large picture frame would work well too.

ABOVE RIGHT: An inexpensive fiberboard table can become a bedside beauty with a slipcover. An inverted pleat, tied with a ribbon adds the perfect tailored touch. This style is easy to make yourself because there is no gathering in the skirt and there is less fabric to work with.

ABOVE: A slipcovered chair provides a contrast to other wooden chairs and sets the host and hostess chairs apart.

RIGHT: These two photos show how one chair can look completely different depending on the slipcover used.

Accessories

Accessories are like the icing on the cake—we want to taste it before the cake has finished baking. Don't be tempted to jump in and accessorize too soon. It's easy to put too many accessories in a room and end up with clutter. Wait until you are finished with the paint, floors, window coverings, and furniture before you jump in with pictures, collectibles, plants, and other accessories.

There are two decorating rules that will help in arranging accessories: Firstly, the Power of Two and The Rule of Three. The Power of Two states that each accessory should be balanced by another that is alike or similar. An example is a pair of candlestick lamps on either end of a buffet table, or matching topiaries on either side of a fireplace mantel. Secondly, the Rule of Three is grouping together in threes, or odd numbers. Often these objects are tied together by color, finish, or subject matter.

When selecting accessories, be certain to arrange them in varying heights to break up the arrangement and make the display more interesting.

Since your home is a reflection of you, use your personal treasures and keepsakes when accessorizing.

TOP RIGHT: Sometimes less is more. The accessories on this mantel illustrate The Power of Two rule. The two candles on the left balance the clock on the right. By keeping accessories to a minimum, the artwork becomes the focal point.

RIGHT: There are several reasons why this tabletop vignette works well. The Rule of Three is used with the three framed vintage family photographs. The fact that the frames have the same finish and the photographs are all black and white helps to tie everything together. If you have a mixture of color and black-and-white photographs to display, consider scanning them to create all black-and-white or sepia tones. The frames are arranged at varying heights for interest and make it easy to see each photograph.

ABOVE: Incorporate treasured items into your decor. The lamp on the table, which once belonged to the home owner's god-mother, was chosen for the guestroom in what she describes as "traditional comfort." Note how the accessories on the table are arranged at varying heights. Books make good risers for elevating accessories.

LEFT: Collections make the best acces-sories in a room because they reflect your passions. This mantel is lined with the home owner's Schumann Dresden china, which also provided the color inspiration for the living-room decor.

Wall Decor

Nothing is as boring as a big white wall. You can banish boring with a good paint color choice and a little ingenuity. There is no need for expensive art if you are willing to be creative. Let your walls tell a story about you and your family. Do you have a collection of small objects that can be framed? If you are a flea market aficionado, a piece of old iron or woodwork can be a great way to add instant character to a wall. Consider adding mantel shelves for dimension and setting treasured objects or framed photographs on them.

Visit a local frame store for ideas to make your own memo board or shadow box. The possibilities are endless, so there is no reason to live with a broad expanse of nothingness on walls.

TOP RIGHT: A piece of chain-link fence cut to fit inside a frame is a creative solution for hanging small sports equipment and awards. Ask your local home improvement store to cut the fencing for you. Be certain to use a pair of pliers to turn back all sharp edges so no one is cut while attaching the fencing to the frame.

BOTTOM: Four inexpensive base-ball bats are attached to the frame of a standard bulletin board. The board is decorated with sports mem-orabilia and can include a favorite jersey and, as in this case, shoes.

RIGHT: Architectural grandeur can be added to a wall by hanging tiles or stepping stones in a geometric arrangement.

BELOW: Antique doors are showcased as a work of art when hung on a wall and accessorized with interesting collectibles.

ABOVE : Colorful glass marbles in varying sizes are glued to a board and framed for a whimsical wall hanging for a game room. Consider using tokens or ticket stubs from memorable events the same way.

ABOVE LEFT: A blank wall can be brought to life with a piece of decorative iron. Wood or metal gates and trellises work well too.

LEFT: A wall shelf with lots of details adds dimension and interest to a wall. Framing special objects such as these two handmade dolls is a good way to display special possessions.

Putting It All Together

Section Two

The Beginning

H ow often have you put off something because you weren't sure where to start? There's no need to avoid decorating for the same reason. True, there are many decisions to be made, but if you break them down and put them in order, you'll find the process fairly simple—and fun.

The starting point for a project depends on the home. One person may be living in a brand new town home with a clean canvas just waiting for paint and area rugs. Another person may have moved into a 1950s tract house with dozens of layers of wallpaper, worn floors, and harvest gold appliances.

To get to a starting point, let's assume you've stripped the walls, patched holes, bared the floors, and removed the window coverings.

Get the Facts

Take accurate measurements of your room. What is the square footage? How high are the walls? How big are the windows? What main elements are in the room? If there is a fireplace, how high is it? How long and deep is the mantel, and what are the hearth dimensions? How high and wide are the doors, and do they open into or out of the room? Record this information in your decorating journal.

Begin working on the furniture placement plan. Get an idea of what pieces you want and where you want to place them.

Making a List and Checking It Twice

A checklist is invaluable to your project. Not only will it keep you focused and organized, it will give you a sense of accomplishment each time you finish something.

CHECKLIST ONE—PRACTICAL THINGS:

☐ Check the electrical outlets. Are there enough? Are they where you want them? If you are going to make any changes, have the electrician add dimmer switches while he/she is there.

☐ Is there enough lighting? If you're going to install additional fixtures, now is the time. It may require making openings in the walls. You aren't going to want to repair newly-painted walls so do it now. Have recessed can lights installed.

☐ Install moldings and millwork. If you're dreaming of crown molding, get it up now so it can be painted when the rest of the room's trim is done.

☐ Have built-in wall or entertainment units installed.

Decisions, Decisions

Now, it's time to choose fabrics, paint, wall coverings, and flooring. An earlier chapter discussed decorating styles. If you haven't decided what yours is—the moment has come. You can't go forward without knowing what look you want—so decide. Once you have your answer, move on to the next list.

CHECKLIST TWO—PRETTY THINGS:

☐ Choose your colors. Decide on the predominant color. Depending on whether you have chosen a complementary, monochromatic, or split complementary color scheme, choose the next colors. If you're having a difficult time with color selection, go to the next item on the checklist.

☐ Choose fabrics. Remember that a color expert has worked with blending and mixing colors when designing the fabric, so often you'll find coordinating and complementary colors are in the fabric design. You just have to choose which ones you want to pull out and use in the room. It's much easier to choose coordinating colors, wood tones, carpet, or other flooring options after you have decided on colors.

☐ Choose flooring. Decide between a carpet, wood, tile, or laminate floor.

Getting Down to Business

Deciding whether to put flooring in before painting or vice versa is like the old chicken-or-the-egg adage—what comes first? If you're installing a wood, tile, or laminate floor, it's best to install it before you paint or wallpaper. The baseboards are installed after this kind of flooring is put in. The baseboards are painted when the rest of the painting is done. It's a safer bet to install carpet after the painting for the obvious reason—you don't want drips ruining your investment.

CHECKLIST THREE—GOING INTO ACTION:

- ☐ Install flooring, then paint or wallpaper the walls. Be certain to protect floors until everything is finished.
- ☐ Finalize furniture choices. Make purchases and schedule deliveries based on your anticipated completion date.
- ☐ Choose window coverings. If you'll be making them yourself time to get to work! If not, order them and set an installation date.
- ☐ Install decorative lighting fixtures.

Almost Done!

The last stages of a decorating project are the most enjoyable because you are seeing how wonderful everything is going to look.

CHECKLIST FOUR—THE FUN PART:

- ☐ Put down area rugs.
- ☐ Arrange furniture.
- ☐ Hang window coverings.
- ☐ Bring in accessories, including plants.
- ☐ Sit back, relax, and enjoy!

Living Rooms

Living rooms have been undergoing an evolution and revolution the last few years. As lifestyles have become more relaxed, so has this traditionally formal room. Generally reserved for entertaining guests, the living room is often off limits to family. With proper planning and furniture placement, the living room can be a welcoming room that is used every day, not just for company.

Consider what other purposes your living room can serve when you don't have guests. If you live in an apartment or small house, a sleeper sofa provides additional sleeping quarters. If you like to read or work on needlework, a corner of the living room can be arranged to be a comfortable getaway from noisier parts of your home.

Home builders are making living rooms smaller based on the belief that people are spending less time in them. If a room is designed well, it can be one of the most comfortable rooms in the house and still be a source of pride when welcoming guests. An overstuffed sofa at the bottom of the staircase makes a great spot for keeping tabs on children while they are in other rooms of the house.

LEFT: The dark armoire anchors this living room and provides a focal point. Hidden behind the wooden doors, the entertainment center gathers both family and friends.

RIGHT: Create small conversation areas within in larger room for a feeling of intimacy.

ABOVE AND RIGHT: A palette of soft, soothing, tone-on-tone fabrics gives this room a spacious feel and optimizes the natural daylight. Off-white pile carpet warms the floors and is the coordinate with formal furniture. The conversation area becomes more intimate with a silk-covered ottoman rather than a coffee table.

First-time Tip

If you aren't in your dream house, but plan to be one day, consider investing in furniture in neutral tones. When you move, the furniture will easily fit in with your new decorating scheme.

ABOVE: A small area rug under a comfortable chair makes this intimate space an ideal place within the larger room to sit and read or spend quiet time. Always include a side table and small reading lamp and leave plenty of surface space open on the table for resting things.

OPPOSITE PAGE: While the overall feel of the room is relaxed, the use of symmetry with the accessories creates a formal undertone.

Living rooms need not to be formal. The room can be lovely, but have a relaxed feel that's sure to be used every day. An area rug over a waxed hardwood floor creates a more relaxed look than wall-to-wall carpet. The area rug defines the seating area and creates a conversation area. Mixing leather and fabric also lends a feeling of casual elegance. Illustrate the Rule of Two by matching lamps on a Bombay chest and adding corbels on the wall with matching urns.

Dining Rooms

I f you are not careful when planning your dining room, it will be a room you hardly use. However, by turning your attention to making it warm and comfortable, you'll want to use it often—regardless of whether or not you are entertaining guests.

A decorative lighting fixture adds ambience to a dining room and can make an attractive focal point. Be certain to have a dimmer installed to create mood lighting.

Table widths are becoming narrower as rooms are shrinking. Be certain to measure enough space for guests to move a chair in and away from the table without bumping into other furniture or walls. If you are apt to be serving meals buffet-style, plan for traffic flow.

Padded chairs are much more comfortable than wooden seats. If you have all-wood chairs, have seat cushions made to match the rest of the room. If you have room for a sideboard or buffet piece, look for one that has drawers for storing flatware and shelves for china and good serving pieces.

When making your final decisions on color and fabrics, be sure you are in love with the choice.

You'll be more likely to use the dining room for everyday meals if you are happy with the decor.

OPPOSITE PAGE: The sturdy design of the dining room table is in contrast with the graceful lines of the host and hostess chairs. Proving that there are few rules in decorating these days, the chairs at the ends of the table are wood, and the guest chairs are upholstered. The stone wall adds an air of aged and rustic beauty to the room, and the round mirror over the buffet echoes the curve in the arched doorway to the kitchen.

BELOW: A comfy area arranged in the corner of the dining room creates a nice spot for after-dinner conversation. The multipurpose room includes a private place to escape the activity of other parts of the house.

High ceilings and clerestory windows can sometimes be a decorating challenge. Choose a hanging light fixture that is big enough for the room. If a fixture is too small, it will get lost because of the spaciousness of the ceiling. Use architectural wall accessories to draw the eye upward and bring an interesting textural element to the room. Tall rooms call for tall furniture, so don't be afraid of heights when decorating these rooms.

ABOVE: Tall architectural elements hung on the wall above the hutch draw the eye upward to the high ceiling.

RIGHT: By mixing a white painted wooden table with natural-stained wooden chairs and using a slipcover on the host and hostess chairs, this dining room becomes relaxed and casual.

First-time Tip

When buying chairs for your home, choose chairs for your other rooms that mix well with your dining-room chairs. That way, when you have extra guests, you can pull in the coordinating chairs from other rooms.

ABOVE: *This classic dining room is kept bright and sunny by choosing a light wood for the hutch, rather than matching all the furniture in darker tones.*

LEFT: *A small relaxed dining room is likely to be used more frequently than a formal one. Woven-back chairs and a glass-topped table are reminiscent of tropical vacation dining.*

Family Rooms

There are as many looks for family rooms as there are family lifestyles. Every family needs a comfortable place to gather and spend time together. When it comes to pleasing everyone at home, comfort has to be the priority. A young child or teenager won't care whether the pillows coordinate with the window coverings, but they will notice if the sofa is comfortable. There should be at least one sofa in this room, and if space permits, consider two. The chair-and-a-half design is great for family rooms as well. An ottoman and a large low table for setting drinks and food are important too. Inevitably the focal point of the room may be an entertainment center. Consider a cabinet with doors to hide the television when not in use.

OPPOSITE PAGE: This large family room is split into two areas—a sitting area and a game area. The hardwood floor under the pool table is practical, while a textured rug softens the conversation area.

BELOW: Overstuffed cushions on sofas and chairs and lots of pillows define comfort in this room. Without the built-in wall unit this family room would be too narrow.

When choosing fabrics for furniture and pillows, be sure it's durable and stain resistant. Most upholstery fabrics are rated for durability, discuss this with a salesperson and take it into consideration when making your choices. Inevitably, someone will end up sitting on the floor while watching television or relaxing, so consider a soft floor covering. Extra oversize pillows will also add to the comfort of the room.

LEFT: In this eclectic family room Tommy Bahama meets The Man in the Gray Flannel Suit. Woven rattan chairs sit opposite two tailored sofas covered in a small houndstooth chenille fabric.

First-time Tip

If you are decorating an entire house at the same time and trying to make your budget stretch as far as possible, consider purchasing living-room furniture that one day can be moved into the family room. This way, when you are able to upgrade the living-room furniture, you'll have great furniture in the family room too.

OPPOSITE PAGE: When the decorator met with this client for the first time, she revealed that her new family room had to withstand use by two young boys, have plenty of storage, and be practical with a feminine touch. Together they chose stain-resistant fabrics and a very durable nylon Berber carpet. A custom-built fireplace surround and cabinets that hide the television and stereo also provide space to store toys.

TOP LEFT: Good lighting, a comfortable chair and ottoman, plus a side table make this a perfect corner for reading. When planning a family room, try to create a spot out of the main traffic area for one person to relax privately.

BOTTOM: Lamps set on a small parson's table behind the sofa provide ample accent lighting. The four floral prints are the focal point behind the sofa and are balanced by the pair of matching lamps.

Home Offices

A home office has become a necessity of life. Whether it is used to run a small business, work after hours at home, or to write letters and pay bills, the home office is one of the most frequently used rooms.

If you work outside the home, it is likely your surroundings are not your own choice. Your home office, on the other hand, is a place where you can have things just the way you like. If you prefer a sleek modern look, now is your chance to express yourself. Or you could be a traditionalist who likes natural woods and overstuffed chairs. Whatever your style, surround yourself with what you love.

One of the important aspects of a home office is that you have plenty of room to spread out. Whether you choose to work on a large table or at a simple workstation, be certain you have enough surface space for the types of projects you will be working on. Good lighting is essential in a home office. You'll need good general lighting—recessed can lights are an excellent option—and task lighting is essential.

Consider the different office machines and computers you will be using, and be certain there are enough electrical outlets. Have any additional

ABOVE: This home office has storage for files and office supplies plus sufficient counter space. A bedroom closet can be removed and a similar system installed if you are converting a bedroom into a home office.

LEFT: Designers say black is the new neutral, and this home-office workspace is proof positive. The black lacquer worktable and counter are simple, elegant, and contemporary. The use of artwork in substantial frames helps balance the room.

OPPOSITE PAGE TOP: Attic or loft space can be converted into a home office. A large dining table makes a good desk and a comfortable chair is ready for visitors and the hardworking home owners. In keeping with the room's decor, the desk chair has been reupholstered in plaid fabric.

OPPOSITE PAGE BOTTOM: Low shelving installed under windows provides storage and an additional work surface for spreading out paperwork.

outlets installed before decorating. Walls may need to be patched and it is much easier to do it before you paint or wallpaper.

Much has been written about the importance of a good desk chair, but until you have experienced the discomfort of a bad one, you may not realize how crucial this is. Forget worrying about aesthetics; posture and comfort will control how effective you are and how long you can sit and work. Remember, you can always have an office desk chair reupholstered or slip-covered to match your decor.

LEFT: This space, with its touch of Hollywood glamour and large, comfy chair, could serve as a den as well as a home office. The amount of file storage, cupboards, and open stationery slots makes it an excellent setup for someone working out of their home. The matching floor lamps provide good overall light and the undercabinet task light encourages productivity at any hour.

BELOW: Any true romantic would love to work in this office. The bright yellow walls complement the black furniture and black-and-white toile curtains. The glass-topped metal table in front of the window is a refreshing companion to the dark, solid wood furniture. Leaving the back off the bookshelf allows the yellow walls to show through and accent the accessories.

ABOVE: Decorative wood moldings—sometimes called overlays—are available on made-to-order cabinets. Many manufacturers offer coordinating corbels, and extra pieces can be ordered. Adding the same overlay to the fireplace surround in an adjacent room is an example of how you can use small accents to tie adjacent rooms together.

OPPOSITE PAGE: A built-in hutch in the breakfast area has the look and feel of antique furniture and provides extra storage for dishes and collectibles. Most major home improvement stores have kitchen cabinet departments that sell similar units made by major furniture manufacturers. You may have to pay a little extra for a custom finish, but it will be less than a custom order.

Kitchens

There is an old adage, "No matter where I serve my guests, they always like my kitchen best." It seems that at even the most formal parties, people seem to gather in the kitchen. If it weren't for the hostess leading her guests into another room, they may just stay there all night.

Since the kitchen is one of the main living areas of a home, it's a decorating priority like other frequently used rooms.

Many first-time decorators shy away from decorating the kitchen because they have heard how expensive it is. Let's straighten out a myth: Renovating a kitchen is expensive, decorating is not. There are many things you can do to an existing kitchen to make it lovely and a pleasure to use.

Just like in a bathroom, good lighting is the first investment you should make. Everything will look better if you replace fluorescent lighting with overhead can lights and decorative fixtures with the right bulbs. A difference is also made when you install task lighting under cabinets.

Here are just a few ideas for decorating a kitchen on a budget.

- Give cabinets a facelift by either restaining or painting them. Buy new knobs and drawer pulls that tie in with your decorating scheme. Don't settle for what you find in home improvement stores; there are better specialty retail and on-line sources for creative cabinet hardware.

- Consider painting the insets of kitchen cabinets a color that contrasts with the rest of the kitchen.

- Create glass-front cabinets by cutting out the cabinet's center panel and replacing it with clear or patterned glass. Remember that if you use clear glass, the cupboards behind the doors should be uncluttered.

- Stencil your favorite quote or saying on a wall to personalize the space.

- Replace a dated kitchen faucet with a newer style.

- If your kitchen appliances are different colors and do not match, have them painted by a professional finisher. You can find companies specializing in painting appliances in the telephone book.

- If your kitchen doesn't have a backsplash behind the counters, install ceramic tile or natural stone. It will instantly upgrade the look of your kitchen.

- Create your own island workspace by placing an interesting antique piece of furniture or an inexpensive steel table with shelving in the center of the kitchen. Hang a light fixture or pot rack over the island.

LEFT: *By using a different stain or wood, the kitchen island stands apart from the cabinets and takes on the feel of a piece of furniture. Recessed can lighting is used generously to assure that there is plenty of light when working anywhere in the kitchen.*

OPPOSITE PAGE ABOVE: *The top cabinets are painted and the bottom ones have a stained wood finish that provides an attractive contrast. Setting the top cabinets on the wall several feet from the ceiling provides a display area and makes the room intimate. The corner cupboard unit and glass-front cabinets on either side of the sink are designer touches widely available from major cabinet manufacturers.*

BELOW: *Using different materials on top of the island and countertops is a good way to save money and keep the decor interesting. Invest in granite for the island surface, and consider composite or laminate materials for other areas.*

OPPOSITE PAGE BELOW: *Whimsical touches—such as using old flatware for drawer and door pulls—are welcome in the kitchen.*

First-time Tip

Add dimension and a custom touch to cabinet fronts with wood appliqués. The embellishments at right are available at hardware stores specializing in furniture refinishing and on-line sales. Appliqués are easily adhered to cabinet fronts and can be painted or stained.

An easy way to enlarge a workspace is to replace the top with a larger counter with an extending round edge where chairs can be pulled up for visiting or eating. Good task lighting under the upper cabinets make counter areas a pleasant place to work.

ABOVE: An all-white kitchen is updated when gray granite countertops and a rich wood floor are part of the scheme. Glass-front upper cabinets add to the retro feel of this kitchen.

RIGHT: *A vintage frame hung from a ribbon adds an element of interest behind the cooktop.*

BELOW: *By positioning the island in the kitchen so it is facing the family room, the cook is able to visit and participate in conversations in the other room. The dark green granite countertop and wooden island dramatically contrast to the cream-colored cabinets.*

A light fixture that doubles as a pot rack is both decorative and practical. The rack's downward lighting is hidden within the design of the metal.

LEFT: A round table was chosen for the eating area because it contrasts and softens the hard lines and angles of other parts of the kitchen. The wall is decorated with a fresco inspired by Italian artwork.

BELOW: The painted wooden table complements the fresco on the facing wall. A whimsical light fixture hangs over the table in a kitchen that any cook would be happy to work in.

ABOVE: *Truly a dream kitchen, the decor of this remodeled space is inspired by the Old World influence of the English Tudor house. An 11' island is the focal point of the kitchen and includes a stainless steel vegetable sink, refrigerator drawers, and roll-out storage drawers.*

LEFT: *The sink and cooking area are close by to make food preparation and cooking easier. A great luxury for a cook is a water spigot over the stove for filling pots. The hood over the range is finished in a slightly darker finish than the cabinets, which adds subtle color interest.*

Media and Game Rooms

Media and game rooms have replaced the bonus rooms of yesterday. Many new homes, particularly in the southern states are being built to include a large room for big-screen televisions and sophisticated sound systems. Once the domain of moguls, movie viewing rooms are becoming commonplace.

Comfortable furniture is imperative, and durability is a must—inevitably eating will be done in a media room. This room should have a kick-your-shoes-off feel that invites relaxing.

Window coverings should have blackout or privacy lining so that light can be blocked out for daytime viewing.

Game rooms are a great place to have fun with carpet designs too.

LEFT: Interior glass doors are a great touch for a media room. Noise from other rooms can be shut out, yet the room still has an open feel. In the case of this room, there is no need to cover the doors because they open to a windowless part of the house where an overabundance of sunlight is not a problem.

ABOVE: Bright multi-colored carpet and simple painted circles on the wall make this game room fun.

ABOVE: While it may be more practical to avoid white in a play room, this colorful swirl can be an inspiration for similar designs.

LEFT: Colored spots for playing a classic game of Twister are inset into the carpet in this game room. Bean bag chairs can be easily moved out of the way when the game begins.

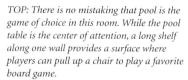

TOP: *There is no mistaking that pool is the game of choice in this room. While the pool table is the center of attention, a long shelf along one wall provides a surface where players can pull up a chair to play a favorite board game.*

ABOVE: *A classic motif from Monopoly is painted on the wall for a happy touch.*

RIGHT: *The Lucky 8 Ball appliquéd on the curtains is made from felt.*

ABOVE: The clean lines of this bedroom make it up-to-date and contemporary. Patterned silk curtains hung from an iron rod with decorative finials are casual yet elegant. The bed style is inspired by a sleigh bed, and its geometric pattern helps set the style for the room.

Bedrooms

Your bedroom is the last thing you see in the evening and the first thing you open your eyes to in the morning, so what better reason to make this room a decorating priority? More time is being spent in bedrooms than ever before. Not only are we sleeping in them, but we're reading, relaxing, exercising, and often working in them.

Every bedroom should have a good reading light, a comfortable reading chair, bedside tables, carpeting or rugs, and window coverings that block out light and maintain privacy.

Indulge yourself by making sure this room reflects your personality. If you have a favorite color, consider painting the walls to suit your pleasure.

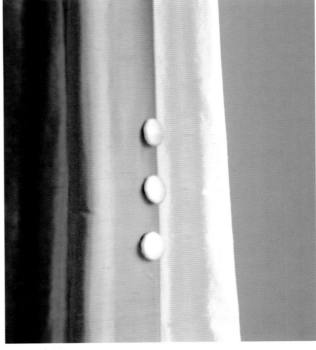

TOP: Attention to detail can make a master bedroom a decorating masterpiece. In this room, layered bedding in coordinating colors and patterns is rich and welcoming. Tassels sewn to the bed skirt are a special touch. Similar tassels may be purchased at most large sewing supply stores in the home decor department.

ABOVE: Decorative pillows embellished with a silk tassel and beaded trim are removed from the bed in the evening and do not take much wear.

RIGHT: Self-covered buttons grouped in threes are a tailored touch on the floor-length curtain.

Themed bedrooms can be very fun to create; and once you have your main idea, you'll find you keep running into fabrics, wallpaper, and accessories that fit in with your plan. This tropical room brings together the texture of grass cloth with hand-painted leaves and ferns on the wall. The window covering is accented with a piece of bamboo. The relaxed style of the slipcover on the desk chair adds to the resort feel of the room.

OPPOSITE PAGE: If you look beyond the luxuriousness of these two bedrooms, you will see that several of the principles of a good bedroom are well illustrated. Each room has a comfortable sitting area and there are table surfaces for working. Placing a bench, chair, or small sofa at the end of a bed provides a comfortable space for putting on shoes or just relaxing.

RIGHT: For an interesting twist, the ceiling is covered with grass-cloth wallpaper.

BELOW: The button-back detail on the chair cover is the type of accent that gives a room a designer touch.

ABOVE: A large frame holds travel memorabilia and is a wonderful way to remember the trip of a lifetime.

LEFT: The window covering combines the textures of cotton fabric trimmed with long threads and a straw shade for a touch of British Colonial style.

RIGHT: With adventure travel as inspiration, this bedroom is filled with creative details. The map, wallpaper, and fabric set the stage. Pockets sewn on the bedspread and pillows bring to mind khaki travel attire, and the round pillow suggests a world globe.

Bathrooms

First-time decorators are generally not in a position to completely renovate a bathroom and incur major plumbing costs. Working with what you have in place and making it attractive and functional is reality. Bathrooms featured in magazines and model homes can be a great inspiration for projects that add designer touches you can do yourself.

Before decorating a bathroom, the best investment you can make is good lighting. No one enjoys looking in the mirror under bad fluorescent lights, so banish it from bathrooms and dressing areas and install good down lighting.

Be certain to plan enough room for plenty of towel bars and hooks when you are working on wall space. A common decorating mistake in bathrooms is to concentrate on a beautiful room that ends up not functioning well due to an oversight on practicalities.

Avoid clutter and keep accessories to a minimum in bathrooms. Good storage for toiletries, towels, and cleaning supplies is essential. If you need additional storage, use a wall-hung shelf unit, a small chest, or a baker's rack.

For a custom look, remove standard construction mirrors and replace with a large framed mirror.

ABOVE: This bathroom shows how fabric hung around the tub softens the room and adds a touch of romance.

OPPOSITE PAGE: This elegant bathroom shows what can be done with great attention to detail and a big budget. The first-time decorator should study rooms like this to glean ideas for their own projects. The built-in window seat provides a comfortable resting place. Lifting the cabinets off the floor with bun feet is an idea that adds a designer touch to any bathroom.

THIS PAGE: These three bathrooms have very different decorating schemes, but share a number of good decorating ideas. Standard mirrors have either been framed or replaced with decorator-style mirrors. General overhead lighting is complemented by decorative lighting, and in the baths with windows, the coverings are a focal point.

First-time Tip

Achieve the look of expensive inlaid tile by using less-costly printed or painted tiles available at home improvement stores.

ABOVE: This elegant bathroom is rich with details including beveled-glass windows, tailored window coverings, inlaid tile along the back of the bathtub, and the backsplashes behind the sinks while glass mosaic tile has been used on the tub surround.

OPPOSITE PAGE: Large museum-sized frames hung on facing walls over dressing vanities are dramatic and grand. Using frames like these in any bathroom will add elegance.

TOP LEFT: Using small color tiles as an accent to white can add a touch of pizzazz to a tub and shower. Home improvement stores sell a variety of accent tiles that can be adhered to existing tiles for color and dimension, making it simple to add interesting detail.

TOP RIGHT: Artwork is a lovely element in the bathroom—just be certain that it is either framed or has been sealed to withstand moisture.

LEFT CENTER AND BOTTOM: Keeping accessories simple and limited in number will prevent a bathroom from looking cluttered and unsightly. Be certain to organize your space so that toiletries or small personal appliances can be stored when not in use.

First-time Tip

An inexpensive way to get the look of a custom mirror is to have a large mirror framed and hung several inches above the sink. Most standard bathroom mirrors are attached to the wall by metal holders at the bottom edge and plastic grips to secure the top. Be sure to have someone help you remove the mirror from the wall.

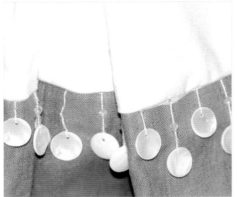

Children's Rooms

The extent some parents go to decorating a child's room makes you wonder if the grown-ups are fulfilling their own childhood fantasies. It's often the one room in the house where money is no object. Yet, durability and adaptability should be key components of the decor. In the blink of an eye, the baby with the sweet nursery will be a preteen balking at what was once cute.

Children's rooms should have plenty of room for storage, a good study place, a comfortable reading area and, if possible, room for guests to sleep.

Choose fabrics that will take heavy wear for bedding and upholstery and save more delicate fabrics for window coverings.

TOP LEFT: A tropical flower motif is stenciled on the walls. A multitude of stencil designs for this simple technique can be purchased at craft stores. When stenciling, use a flat stencil brush and very little paint. The paint on the brush should be almost dry so it will not drip down the wall after it is applied.

BOTTOM LEFT: The beaded trim with mother-of-pearl disks used on the bed skirt adds to the beach theme of this room.

ABOVE: Teenagers will enjoy a room that reflects their interests. Three surfboards of varying heights make a fun headboard in a tropical-themed room. The heavy cotton duvet will withstand much wear and brings color to the room. A comfortable chair is an important component of any child's room.

TOP RIGHT: The teardrop valance is tied with bows to an upholstered rod with rosette finials. Each teardrop is piped in rose-colored fabric and trimmed with a hanging crystal.

BELOW: Designed for a four-year-old girl, this room will move with her well into her teenage years. The walls are painted a yellow harlequin pattern and accented in a berry color for a look that is sophisticated and fun. The pair of painted wooden sleigh beds makes a place for a special overnight guest.

Many grandparents are creating fantasy children's rooms in their homes for visiting grandchildren. There is no better enticement for grandchildren to spend time with grandparents than to have their own room when visiting. When decorating the room, grandmother may want to include a special sitting area where she can slip away when the children are not visiting.

ABOVE: This delightful room—measuring only 12' x 13'—was inspired by a French street scene. A hand-painted mural incorporates the granddaughter's names. The café theme is evident in the awning-style valance over the window and the table and chairs that look like they came right off a Paris sidewalk.

RIGHT: The homeowner already owned the settee and wicker chest. The settee was reupholstered and the chest repainted. If you have pieces you like, but they don't fit into your decorating plan, visualize them in different colors, fabrics, or finishes. You'll often find they can be reborn into exactly what you need for your project.

ABOVE: This whimsical chair sets the tone of the room and is a comfortable resting spot because of its high back and well-padded arms.

TOP LEFT: A visit to The Butterfly House during a summer trip to Mackinac Island was the inspiration for this young girl's room. The ceiling and walls were painted soft sky blue, and clouds were painted from floor to ceiling to resemble the outdoors. The built-in unit was painted in bright colors to match the plaid fabric bedding. Butterflies are aflutter on the walls and window covering.

BOTTOM LEFT: The "Flower Power" birthday party invitation to a daughter's eighth birthday celebration set the decorating theme for this bright, high-energy room. The green glazed walls, pink chenille bedspread, and vinyl cornice boxes over the windows reflect the colorful '60s era. There is plenty of room for playing on the floor, a comfortable reading chair, and a vanity that was specifically requested by the young miss for the room.

A child's bed is bound to take heavy wear from playing and sitting with friends, so chenille is a good choice for the spread. Fun details like the ball trim used on the edges of the spread, the fabric vanity cover, and for the curtain tiebacks are in places that will not be constantly touched.

Acknowledgments

Special thanks to the following people and companies. Their helpful spirit made this book possible:

INTERIORS by Decorating Den
www.Decorating Den.com
1-800-DEC-DENS

Carol Donarye Bugg, ASID, DDCD
Vice-President and Director of Design, for her advice on choosing a decorator.

The following decorators from INTERIORS by Decorating Den:

Marg Anquetil, DDCD–47 bottom right, 114 top right

Sharon Binkerd–8, 112, 114 top left, 117 bottom left

Tonya Comer–4, 5 lower, 14 top right, 16 left, 60 top

Joyce Doebler–16 right, 52, 95

Terri Ervin–65, 71

Christine Gritzan–24 bottom

Melanie Jakab–48 top right

Catherine Lloyd–33 top, 97 top

Bonnie Pressley, Allied ASID, DDCD–120

Suzanne Price–121 bottom left

Susan Quattrociocchi–76–77

Kristi Roberson–93

Carolyn Ryberg–100–101

Rebecca Shearn, Allied ASID–24 top, 42, 47 top left, 50, 54 bottom, 56 right, 113, 114 bottom right, 117 top right, 119, 123 right

Judith Slaughter, Allied ASID, DDCD–74, 75, 96

Connie Thompson–62

Judy Underwood, Allied ASID–51

Joanne Watson–88, 89

Cliff Welles, ASID–51

Also by INTERIORS by Decorating Den–60 bottom, 121 top left and right

Shea Homes
For allowing us to photograph model homes in Costa Mesa and San Clemente, California, www.sheahomes.com

Pacific Dimensions, Inc.
Designer of the model homes at Renaissance and The Reserve South. (310) 335-1800

Interior Life Styles, Inc. - Annamaria Neihoff
Designer of the model homes at Traditions and The Reserve North. (714) 434-2858

KraftMaid Cabinetry, Inc.
Cabinet accessory images, www.kraftmaid.com

Plaid Enterprises, Inc.
Gallery Glass, www.plaidonline.com

Style Solutions
Miterless corners, ceiling medallion, www.stylesolutions.com

Laurell Bertino
Laurell Bertino Interiors (949) 831-9790
Pages 2, 3, 9, 18, 20, 25, 126.

Deanne Carey
Lighting Expert

INTERIORS by Decorating Den
4, 5 bottom, 8, 24, 33, 42, 47 top right and lower right, 48 top right, 50, 51, 52, 54 bottom, 56 right, 60 bottom, 61 top, 65, 71, 74, 75, 76, 77, 88, 89, 93, 95, 96, 97 top, 100, 101, 112, 113, 114, 117 bottom left and right, 119, 120, 121, 123 right

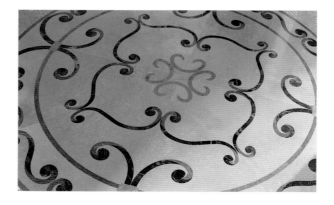

Photo Credits

Wanelle Fitch

Wanelle Fitch Photography (949) 673-8173

Cover, 3, 5, 10–12, 14–15, 17, 21, 27, 30, 32, 34–36, 35 right, 40–41, 43–45, 47 top left and bottom left, 48 top left, 55, 56 bottom, 57–59, 61 bottom, 62, 64, 72–73, 78–79, 82, 86, 91, 98–99, 102, 104 left, 105–107, 108, 109–111, 115–116, 117 top left and center left, 118, 122, 123 left.

Mayer & Bowden Photography

Long Beach, CA (562) 434-1420

Pages 28–29, 31, 35 left, 53, 60 top, 80, 81, 83–85, 90, 92, 103, 104, right, 109.

Mark Tanner

Mark Tanner Photography,
Los Angeles, CA (323) 227-6292

Pages 2–3, 9, 18, 20, 25, 126.

Michael Skarsten

Salt Lake City, UT (801) 359-5515

Page 69 left and middle right.

Index

About the Author

The Author

Eileen Cannon Paulin has been fascinated with interior decorating from the moment the first bedroom she can remember was painted pink and Priscilla curtains were hung. Her lifelong passion for writing and decorating has inspired the launch of Red Lips 4 Courage Communications a creative services company specializing in publications by, about, and for women of all ages. Red Lips recognizes the woman who cherishes family and friends, creates a loving home and enjoys the soft and sentimental side of life.

Eileen appears regularly on HGTV and The Discovery Channel, and is a frequent guest on "It's Christopher Lowell!" She is the former editor of Romantic Homes magazine and the former associate publisher of Victorian Homes magazine. Eileen is the author of "The Serene Home" (Sterling Publishing, 2003).

Metric Conversion

mm-millimeters cm-centimeters
inches to millimeters and centimeters

inches	mm	cm	inches	cm	inches	cm
1/8	3	0.3	9	22.9	30	76.2
1/4	6	0.6	10	25.4	31	78.7
1/2	13	1.3	12	30.5	33	83.8
5/8	16	1.6	13	33.0	34	86.4
3/4	19	1.9	14	35.6	35	88.9
7/8	22	2.2	15	38.1	36	91.4
1	25	2.5	16	40.6	37	94.0
1 1/4	32	3.2	17	43.2	38	96.5
1 1/2	38	3.8	18	45.7	39	99.1
1 3/4	44	4.4	19	48.3	40	101.6
2	51	5.1	20	50.8	41	104.1
2 1/2	64	6.4	21	53.3	42	106.7
3	76	7.6	22	55.9	43	109.2
3 1/2	89	8.9	23	58.4	44	111.8
4	102	10.2	24	61.0	45	114.3
4 1/2	114	11.4	25	63.5	46	116.8
5	127	12.7	26	66.0	47	119.4
6	152	15.2	27	68.6	48	121.9
7	178	17.8	28	71.1	49	124.5
8	203	20.3	29	73.7	50	127.0

yards to meters

yards	meters	yards	meters	yards	meters	yards	meters	yards	meters
1/8	0.11	2 1/8	1.94	4 1/8	3.77	6 1/8	5.60	8 1/8	7.43
1/4	0.23	2 1/4	2.06	4 1/4	3.89	6 1/4	5.72	8 1/4	7.54
3/8	0.34	2 3/8	2.17	4 3/8	4.00	6 3/8	5.83	8 3/8	7.66
1/2	0.46	2 1/2	2.29	4 1/2	4.11	6 1/2	5.94	8 1/2	7.77
5/8	0.57	2 5/8	2.40	4 5/8	4.23	6 5/8	6.06	8 5/8	7.89
3/4	0.69	2 3/4	2.51	4 3/4	4.34	6 3/4	6.17	8 3/4	8.00
7/8	0.80	2 7/8	2.63	4 7/8	4.46	6 7/8	6.29	8 7/8	8.12
1	0.91	3	2.74	5	4.57	7	6.40	9	8.23
1 1/8	1.03	3 1/8	2.86	5 1/8	4.69	7 1/8	6.52	9 1/8	8.34
1 1/4	1.14	3 1/4	2.97	5 1/4	4.80	7 1/4	6.63	9 1/4	8.46
1 3/8	1.26	3 3/8	3.09	5 3/8	4.91	7 3/8	6.74	9 3/8	8.57
1 1/2	1.37	3 1/2	3.20	5 1/2	5.03	7 1/2	6.86	9 1/2	8.69
1 5/8	1.49	3 5/8	3.31	5 5/8	5.14	7 5/8	6.97	9 5/8	8.80
1 3/4	1.60	3 3/4	3.43	5 3/4	5.26	7 3/4	7.09	9 3/4	8.92
1 7/8	1.71	3 7/8	3.54	5 7/8	5.37	7 7/8	7.20	9 7/8	9.03
2	1.83	4	3.66	6	5.49	8	7.32	10	9.14